Duets for Christmas

DAN COATES

POPULAR PIANO LIBRARY

Since 1976, Dan Coates has arranged thousands of popular music titles. Composers and artists such as John Williams, Burt Bacharach, and Elton John have expressed total confidence in Dan's ability to create outstanding piano arrangements that retain the essence of the original music. He has arranged everything from movie, television, and Broadway themes to chart-topping pop and rock titles. In addition to creating piano arrangements for players of all levels, Dan also composes original music for student pianists.

The duets in this series capture a variety of styles and provide valuable experiences in developing listening skills, technique, and musicianship. They are arranged for one piano, four hands, with the *primo* and *secondo* parts on separate, facing pages. Measure numbers are provided for easy reference, while suggestions for fingering and dynamics help prepare students for rehearsals and performances. These pieces are excellent crowd-pleasers that are perfect for recitals, encores, piano ensemble classes—or just plain fun.

CONTENTS

Produced by
Alfred Music
P.O. Box 10003
Van Nuys, CA 91410-0003
alfred.com

Printed in USA.

ISBN-10: 0-7390-9361-4
ISBN-13: 978-0-7390-9361-0

Cover Image
Christmas still life: © Shutterstock / Jag_cz

Believe

(from *The Polar Express*)

SECONDO

Words and Music by
ALAN SILVESTRI and GLEN BALLARD
Arranged by Dan Coates

Moderately slow

Believe

(from *The Polar Express*)

PRIMO

Words and Music by
ALAN SILVESTRI and GLEN BALLARD
Arranged by Dan Coates

Moderately slow

Both hands 8va higher throughout

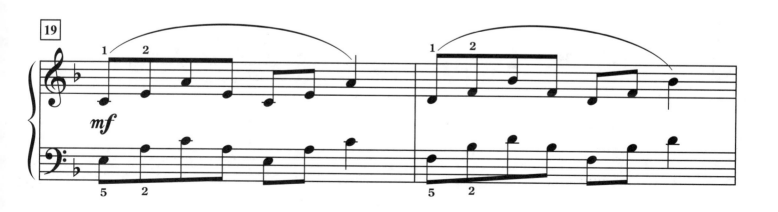

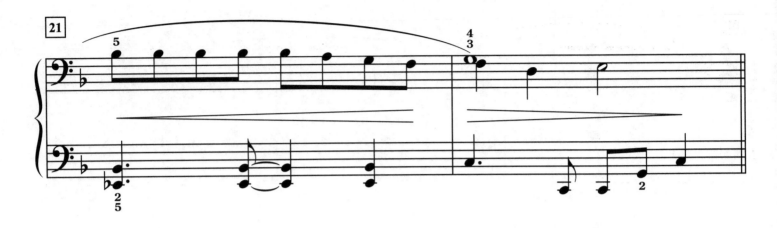

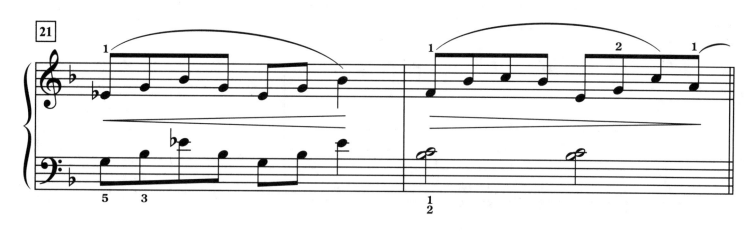

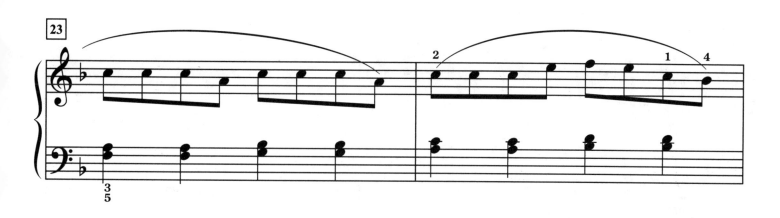

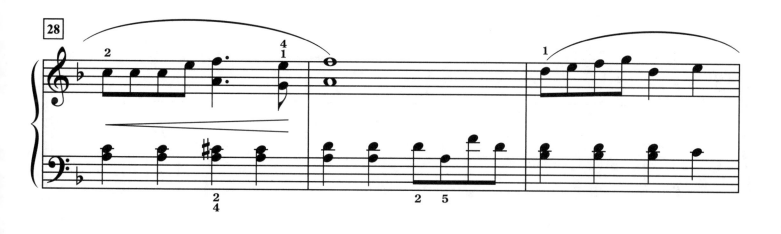

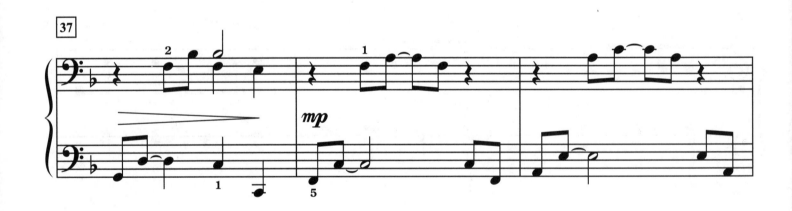

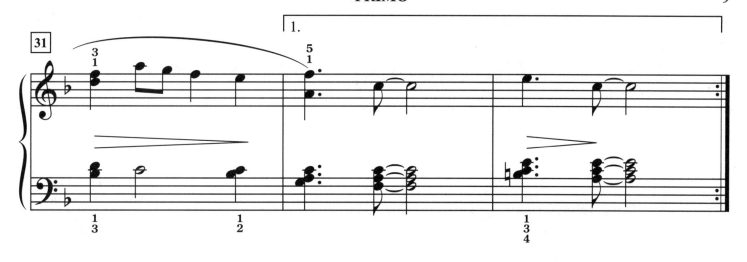

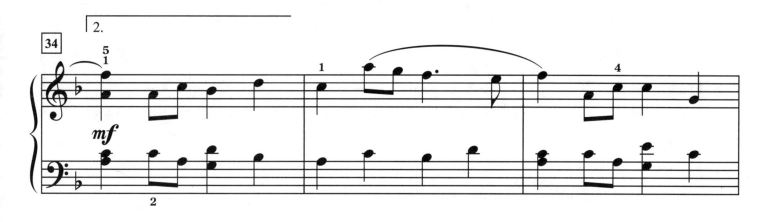

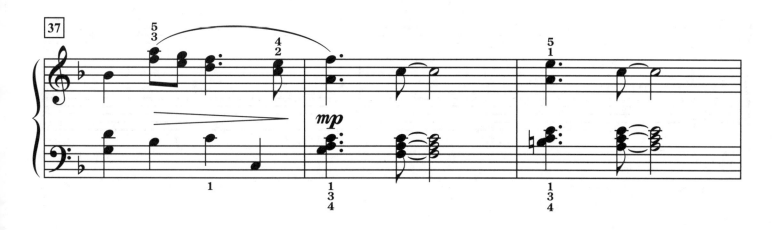

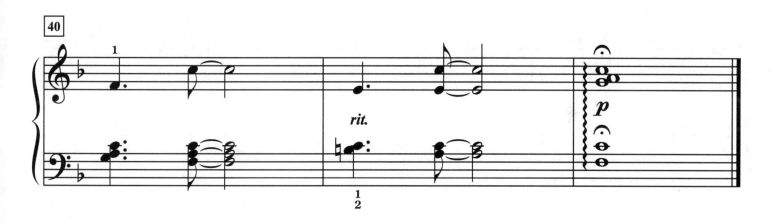

The Christmas Waltz

SECONDO

Words by SAMMY CAHN
Music by JULE STYNE
Arranged by Dan Coates

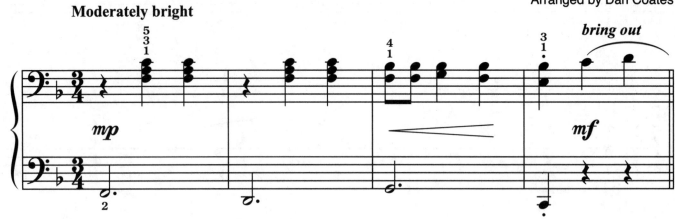

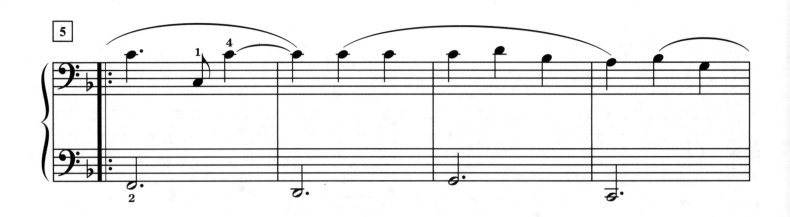

The Christmas Waltz

PRIMO

Words by SAMMY CAHN
Music by JULE STYNE
Arranged by Dan Coates

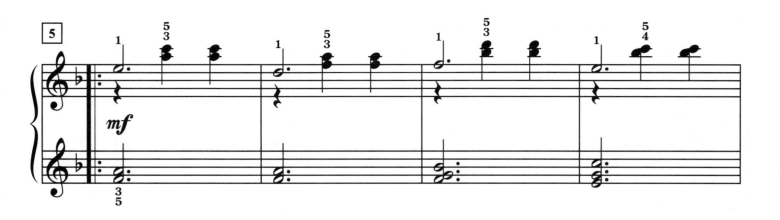

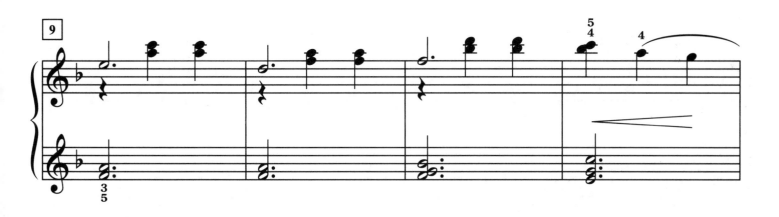

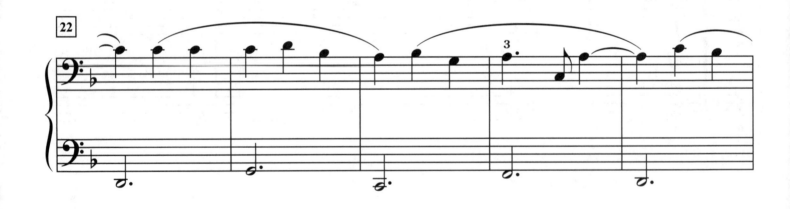

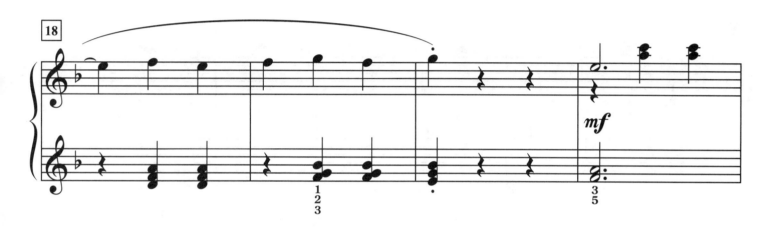

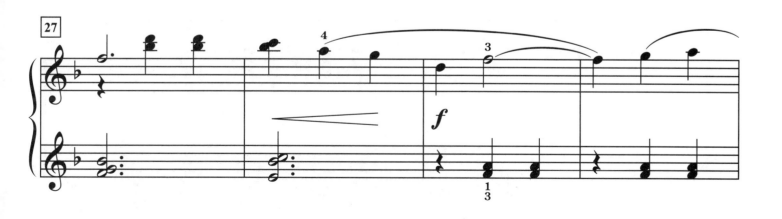

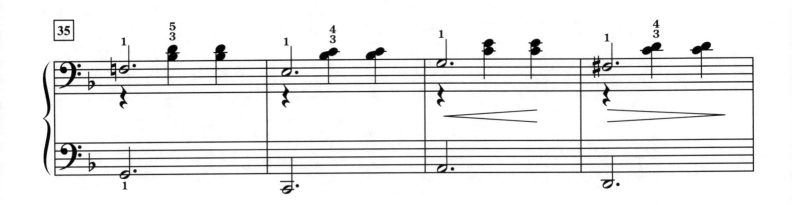

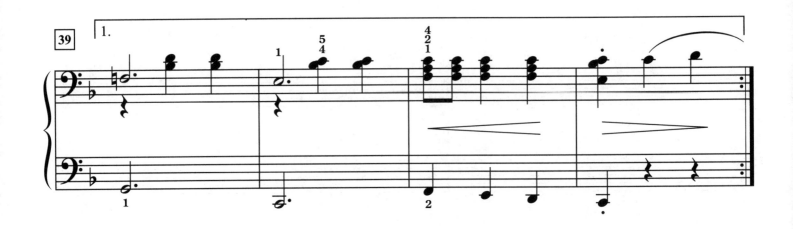

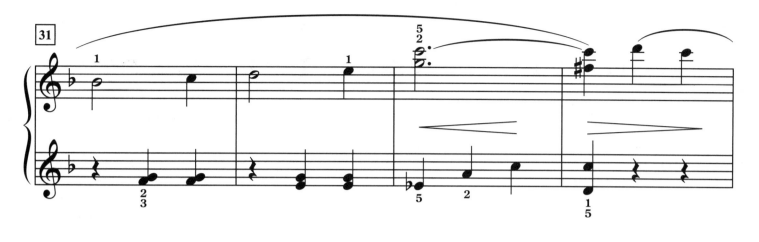

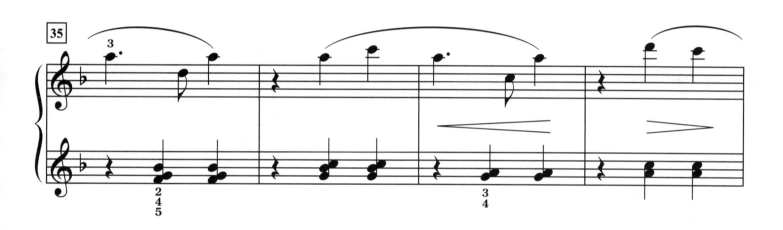

Have Yourself a Merry Little Christmas

SECONDO

Words and Music by
HUGH MARTIN and RALPH BLANE
Arranged by Dan Coates

Have Yourself a Merry Little Christmas

PRIMO

Words and Music by
HUGH MARTIN and RALPH BLANE
Arranged by Dan Coates

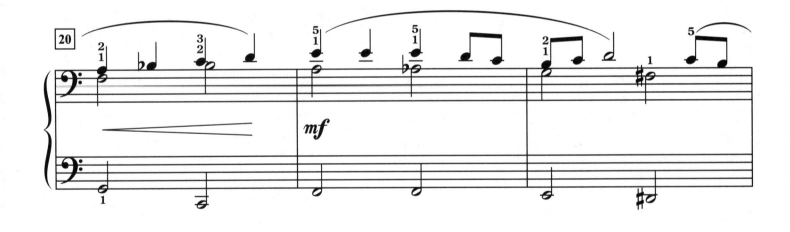

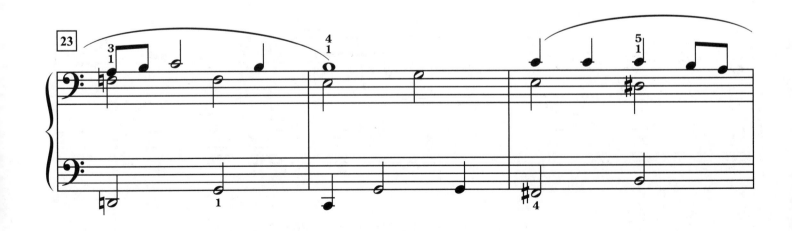

A Holly Jolly Christmas

SECONDO

Words and Music by
JOHNNY MARKS
Arranged by Dan Coates

A Holly Jolly Christmas

PRIMO

Words and Music by
JOHNNY MARKS
Arranged by Dan Coates

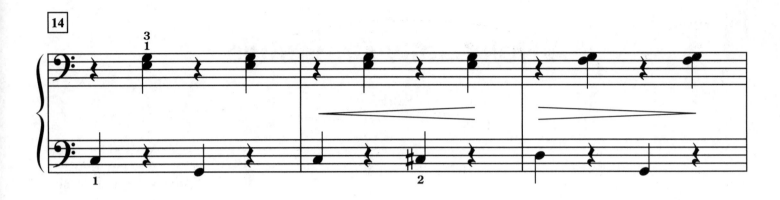

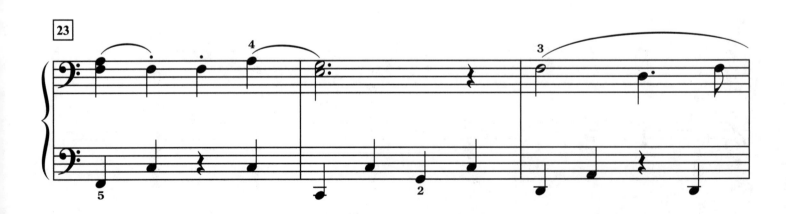

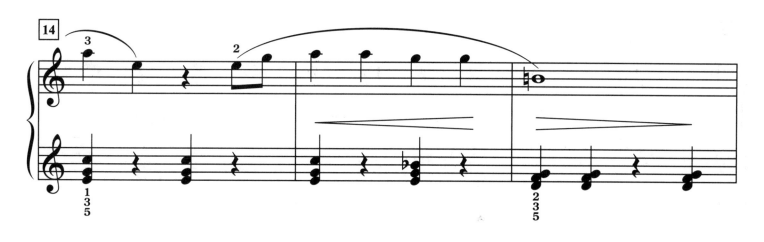

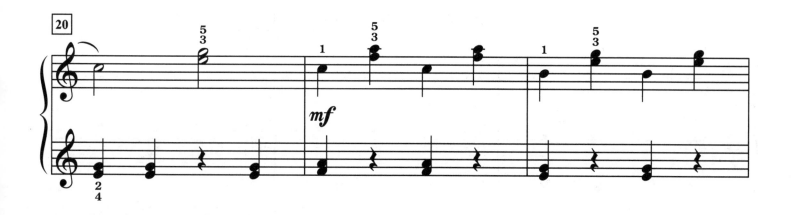

I'll Be Home for Christmas

SECONDO

Words by KIM GANNON
Music by WALTER KENT
Arranged by Dan Coates

I'll Be Home for Christmas

PRIMO

Words by KIM GANNON
Music by WALTER KENT
Arranged by Dan Coates

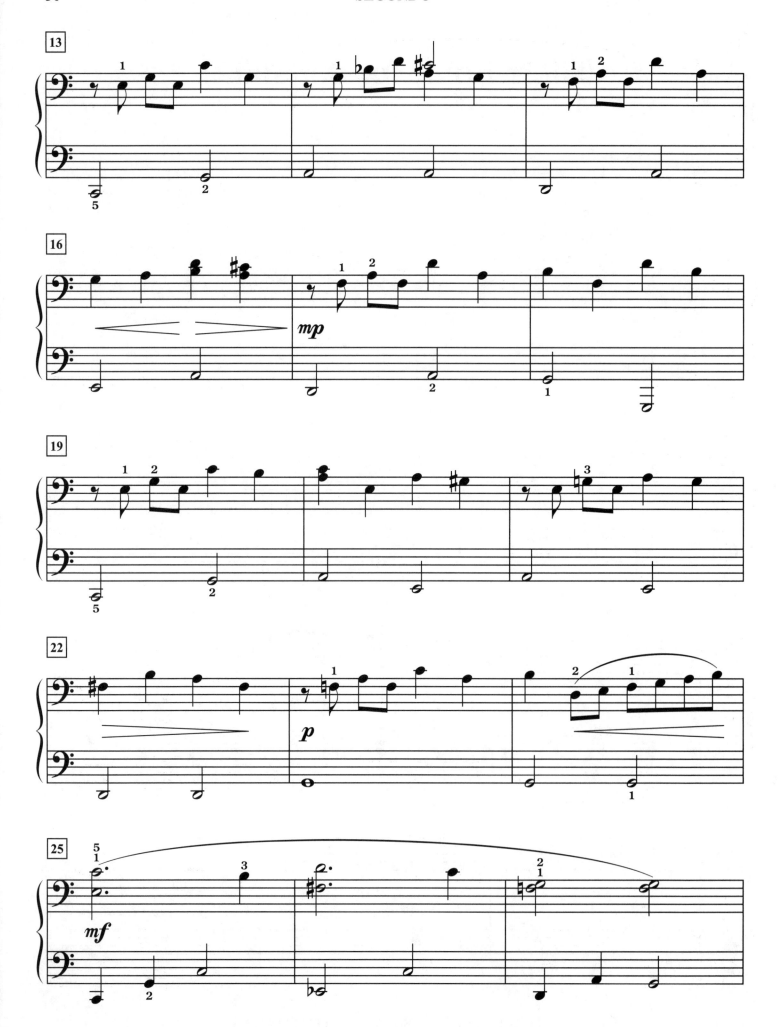

O Holy Night

SECONDO

Words by PLACIDE CAPPEAU
Music by ADOLPHE C. ADAM
Arranged by Dan Coates

Slowly, with expression

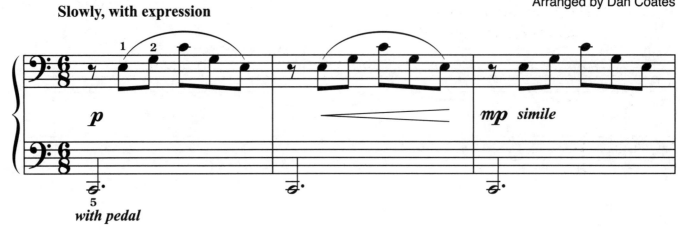

with pedal

O Holy Night

PRIMO

Words by PLACIDE CAPPEAU
Music by ADOLPHE C. ADAM
Arranged by Dan Coates

Slowly, with expression
Both hands 8va higher throughout

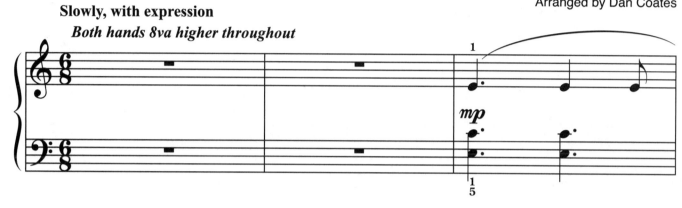

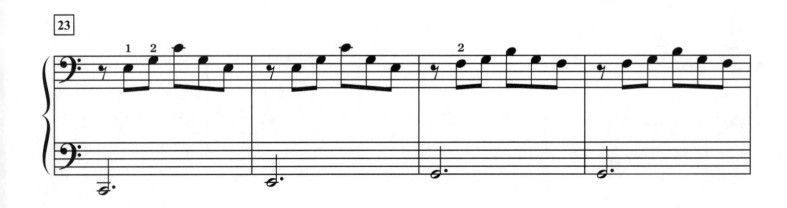

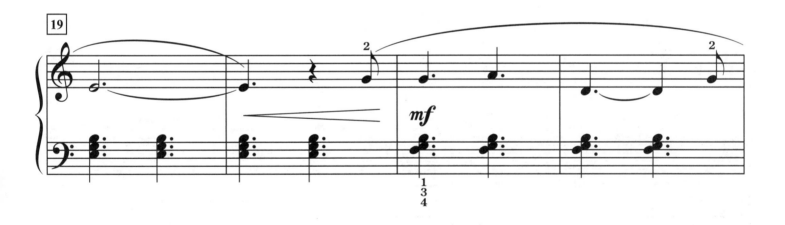

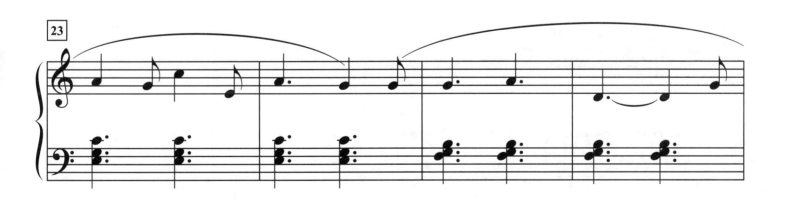

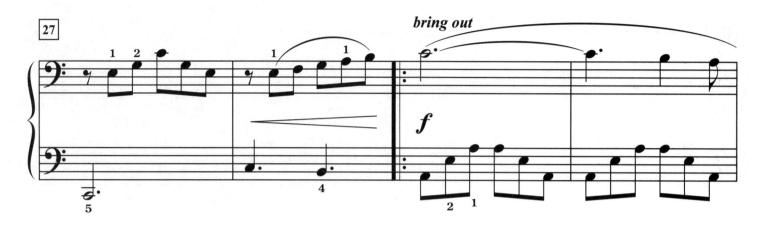

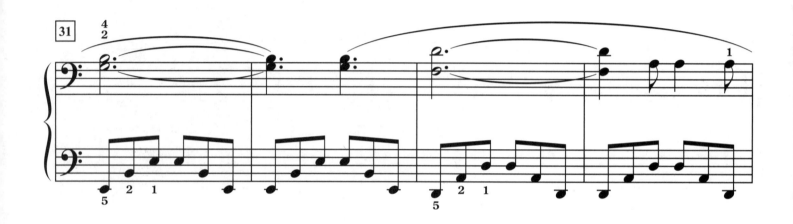

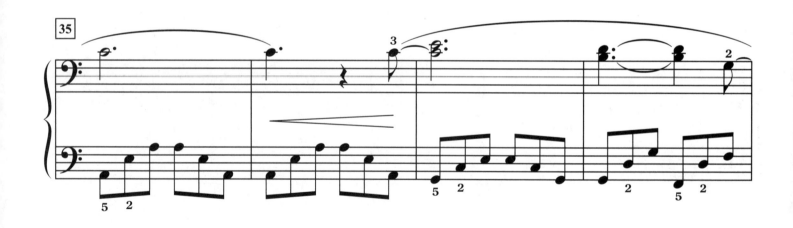

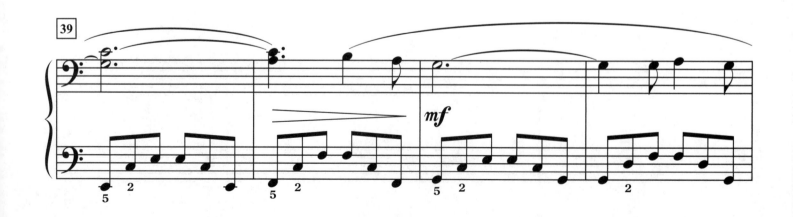

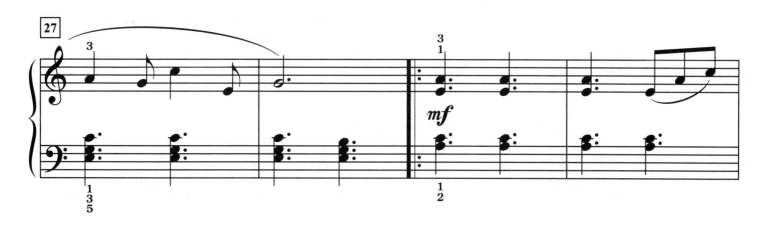

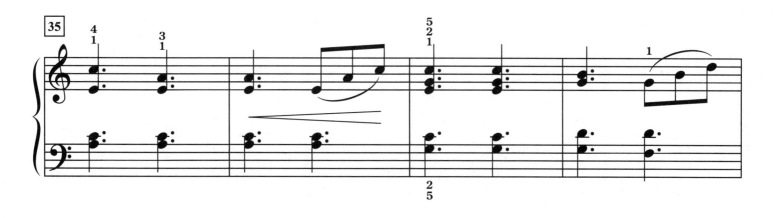

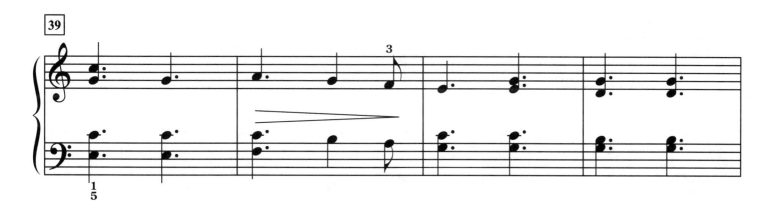

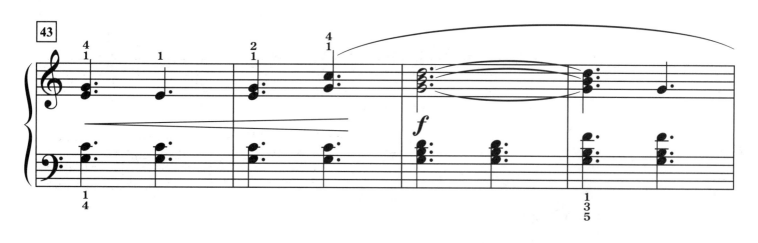

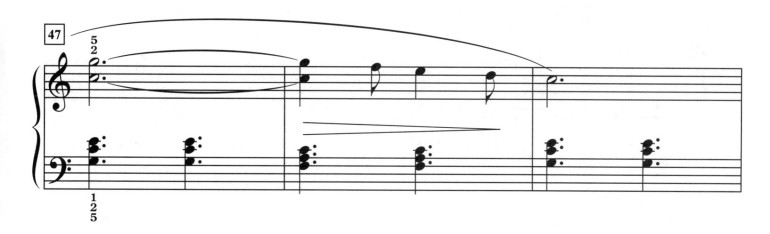

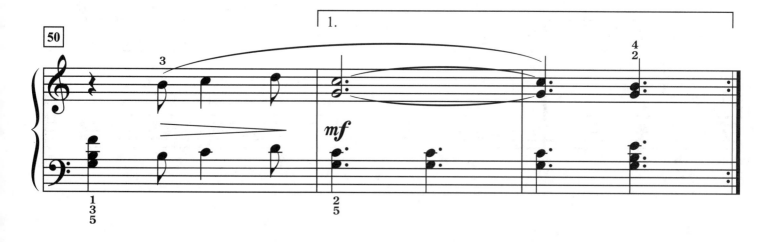

Sleigh Ride

SECONDO

By LEROY ANDERSON
Arranged by Dan Coates

Moderately bright

Sleigh Ride

PRIMO

By LEROY ANDERSON
Arranged by Dan Coates

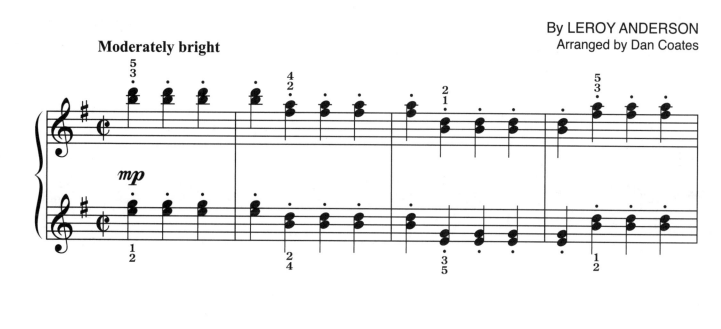

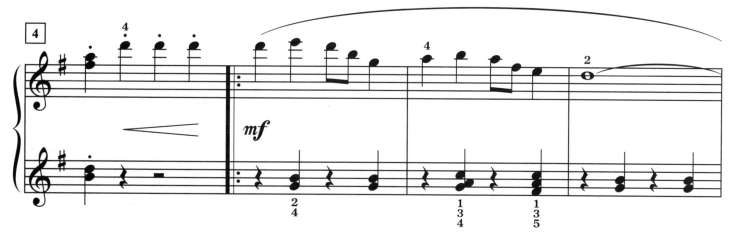

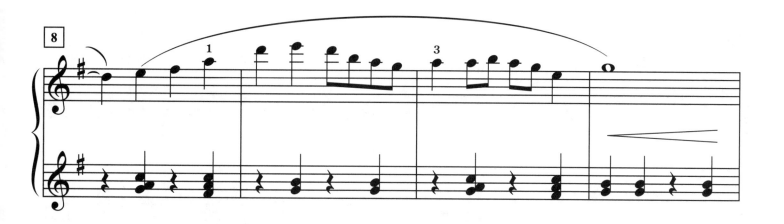

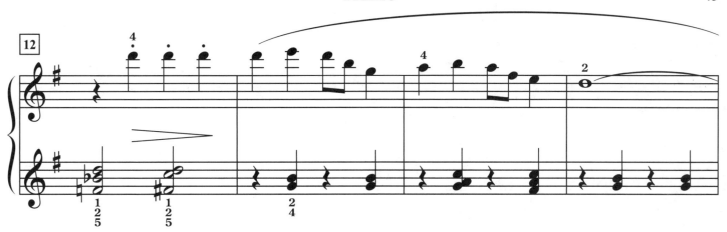

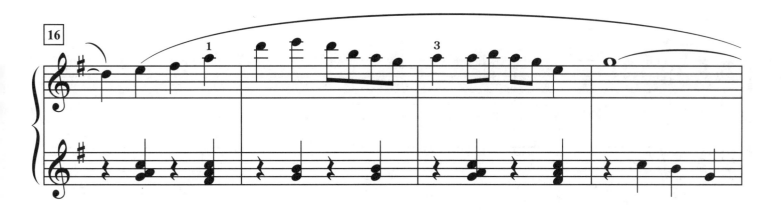

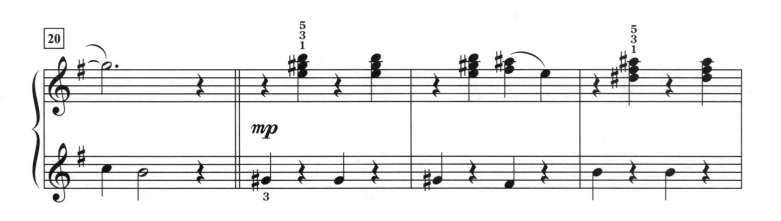

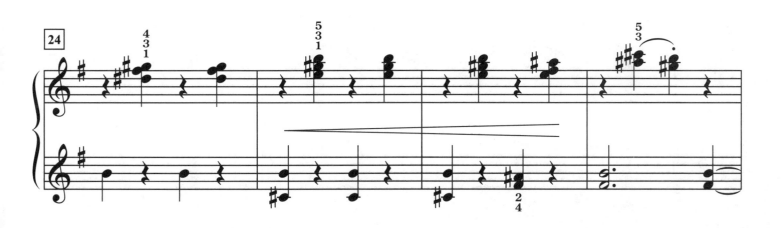

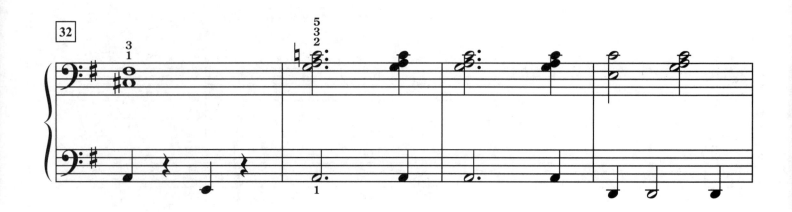

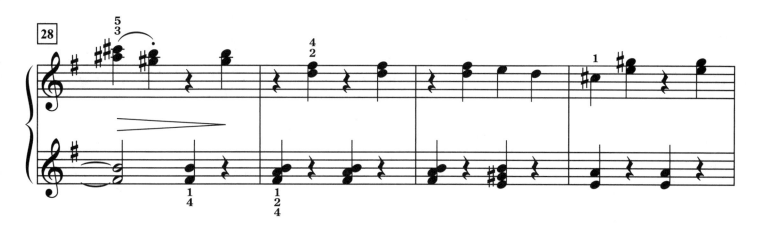

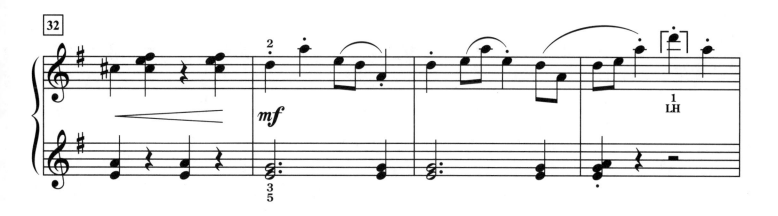

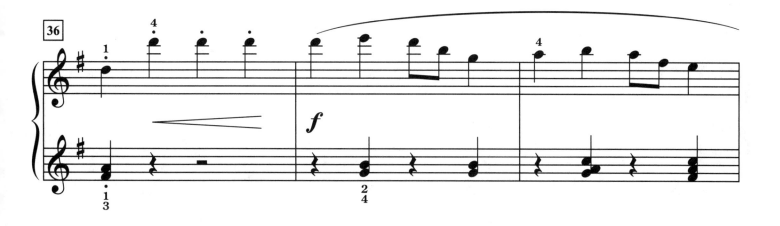

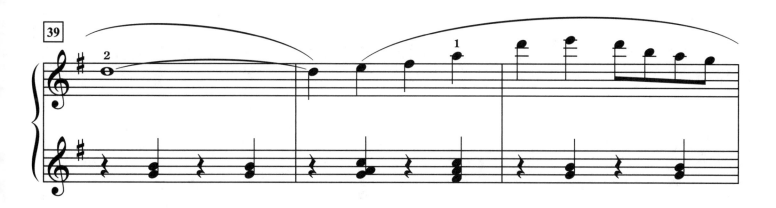

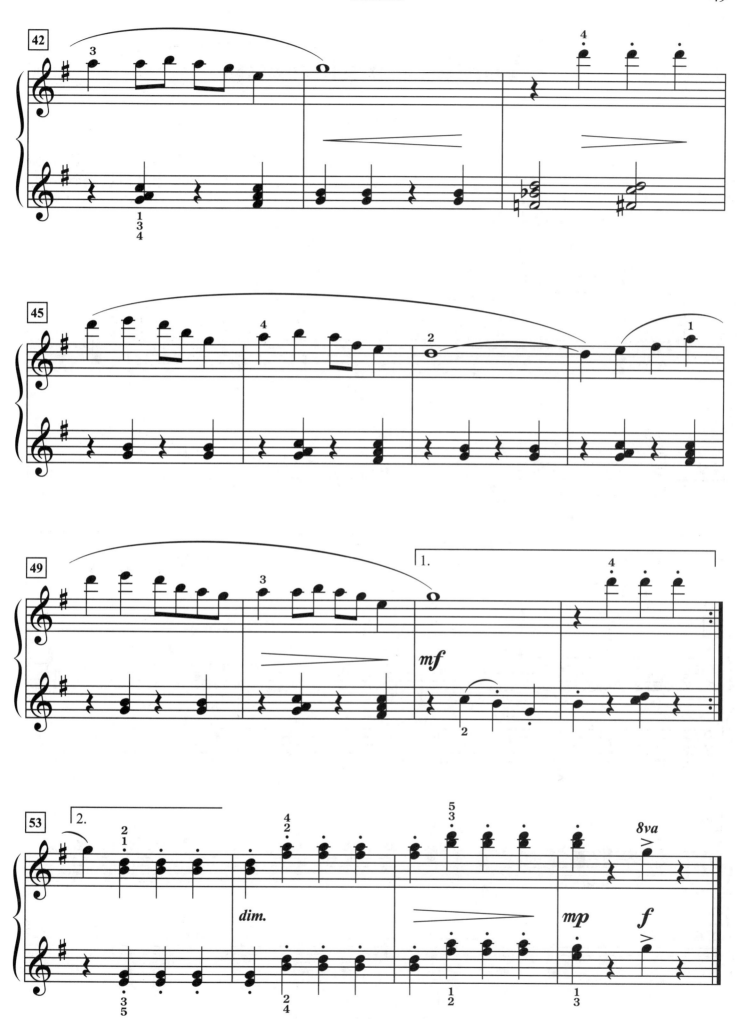

Winter Wonderland

SECONDO

Words by DICK SMITH
Music by FELIX BERNARD
Arranged by Dan Coates

Winter Wonderland

PRIMO

Words by DICK SMITH
Music by FELIX BERNARD
Arranged by Dan Coates

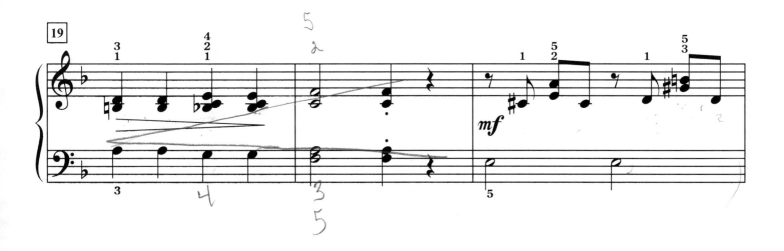

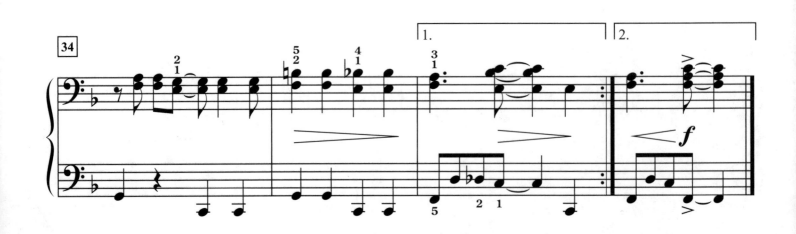